KING COBRA VS. MONGOOSE

BY KIERAN DOWNS

BELLWETHER MEDIA • MINNEAPOLIS, MN

T0020309

TM

Torque brims with excitement
perfect for thrill-seekers of all kinds.
Discover daring survival skills, explore
uncharted worlds, and marvel at mighty
engines and extreme sports. In *Torque* books,
anything can happen. Are you ready?

This edition first published in 2022 by Bellwether Media, Inc.

No part of this publication may be reproduced in whole or in part without written permission of the publisher. For information regarding permission, write to Bellwether Media, Inc., Attention: Permissions Department, 6012 Blue Circle Drive, Minnetonka, MN 55343.

Library of Congress Cataloging-in-Publication Data

Names: Downs, Kieran, author.
Title: King cobra vs. mongoose / by Kieran Downs.
Description: Minneapolis, MN : Bellwether Media, 2022. | Series: Torque:
   Animal battles | Includes bibliographical references and index. |
   Audience: Ages 7-12 | Audience: Grades 4-6 | Summary: "Amazing
   photography accompanies engaging information about the fighting
   abilities of king cobras and mongooses. The combination of high-interest
   subject matter and light text is intended for students in grades 3
   through 7"– Provided by publisher.
Identifiers: LCCN 2021001455 (print) | LCCN 2021001456 (ebook) | ISBN
   9781644875339 (library binding) | ISBN 9781648344954 (paperback) | ISBN
   9781648344411 (ebook)
Subjects: LCSH: King cobra–Juvenile literature. | Mongooses–Juvenile
   literature.
Classification: LCC QL666.064 D69 2022 (print) | LCC QL666.064 (ebook) |
   DDC 597.96/42–dc23
LC record available at https://lccn.loc.gov/2021001455
LC ebook record available at https://lccn.loc.gov/2021001456

Editor: Rebecca Sabelko   Designer: Josh Brink

Printed in the United States of America, North Mankato, MN.

TABLE OF CONTENTS

THE COMPETITORS 4

SECRET WEAPONS 10

ATTACK MOVES 16

READY, FIGHT! 20

GLOSSARY 22

TO LEARN MORE 23

INDEX 24

THE COMPETITORS

The jungles of Southeast Asia are home to some dangerous animals. King cobras are among the most dangerous. These royal **reptiles** pack deadly bites.

But king cobras have a tough challenger. Mongooses are **mammals** known to eat cobras. Who would win in a battle between these two **fierce** fighters?

KING COBRA PROFILE

LENGTH
UP TO 18 FEET
(5.5 METERS)

WEIGHT
UP TO 20 POUNDS
(9 KILOGRAMS)

| 0 | 5 FEET | 10 FEET | 15 FEET | 20 FEET |

HABITAT

RAIN FORESTS

SWAMPS

KING COBRA RANGE

RANGE

King cobras are found in southern and southeastern Asia. They live in warm areas with high **humidity**, often near water.

King cobras are the largest **venomous** snakes in the world! They can reach up to 18 feet (5.5 meters) long. They can be yellow, green, brown, or black. Yellow or white bands run across their bodies.

There are 33 different types of mongoose. They are found in Africa, southern Asia, and southern Europe. They are an **invasive species** on many islands.

Mongooses have short legs, pointed noses, and small ears. They have long, slim bodies and furry tails. Their fur is usually gray or brown.

THROWING FOOD

Mongooses are known to throw eggs at rocks to break open the shells!

INDIAN GRAY MONGOOSE PROFILE

LENGTH
UP TO 2.7 FEET
(0.8 METERS)

WEIGHT
9 POUNDS
(4 KILOGRAMS)

| 0 | 1 FOOT | 2 FEET | 3 FEET |

HABITAT

GRASSLANDS   FORESTS   SCRUBLAND

INDIAN GRAY MONGOOSE RANGE

☐ RANGE

SECRET WEAPONS

KING COBRA FANG

AROUND 0.5 INCHES (13 MILLIMETERS)

King cobras have two short **fangs** in their mouths. Their fangs measure about 0.5 inches (13 millimeters) long. They point back in their mouths. This helps cobras swallow their **prey** whole.

Mongooses' mouths are lined with sharp teeth. They snap down on their prey with powerful jaws. Mongoose bites can do a lot of damage.

King cobras have **glands** that produce a deadly venom. They **inject** the venom through their fangs when they bite prey. The venom makes prey stop breathing.

STRONG VENOM

The amount of venom that a king cobra can deliver in one bite is enough to take down an elephant!

MONGOOSE

SHARP TEETH

STRONG JAWS

VENOM
RESISTANCE

SPEED

Mongooses can **resist** snake venom.
They have a special **antivenom** in their
bodies. It weakens the effect of the venom.

SECRET WEAPONS

ANGLED FANGS

DEADLY VENOM

WIDE HOOD

King cobras spread their ribs to create a **hood**. The hood makes the snakes look larger and more dangerous.

Mongooses are fast! They can chase prey at 20 miles (32 kilometers) per hour. But their speed really shines in a showdown. They dodge attacks and strike back with ease.

MONGOOSE TOP SPEED

20 MILES (32 KILOMETERS) PER HOUR

INDIAN GRAY MONGOOSE

28 MILES (45 KILOMETERS) PER HOUR

HUMAN

ATTACK MOVES

STANDING TALL

King cobras can raise their bodies up to 4 feet (1.2 meters) off the ground!

When king cobras are cornered, they get ready to attack. They raise the front of their bodies off the ground, open their hoods, and hiss. This often scares enemies away.

Mongooses often take their time in fights.
They use their **stamina** to tire out enemies.
Fights can last up to an hour!

King cobras attack with fast strikes. They **lash** out at high speeds to bite their prey. Then they snap back and get ready for another strike.

Mongooses strike when their enemies are tired. They attack with a fast bite to the back of the head. One bite is usually enough!

READY, FIGHT!

A mongoose approaches a king cobra. The snake tries to escape. But it is cornered! It rises off the ground and opens its hood. But the mongoose does not back down.

The cobra bites the mongoose. But the mongoose is not hurt! It sinks its teeth into the cobra's head. The snake just became the mongoose's meal!

GLOSSARY

antivenom—a substance that acts against the effects of venom

fangs—long, sharp teeth

fierce—strong and intense

glands—parts of the body that make a substance

hood—the expanded neck of a cobra

humidity—the amount of wetness in the air

inject—to force a fluid into something

invasive species—a species that is not originally from a region and causes harm to its new environment

lash—to move quickly and suddenly

mammals—warm-blooded animals that have backbones and feed their young milk

prey—animals that are hunted by other animals for food

reptiles—cold-blooded animals that have backbones and lay eggs

resist—to be able to hold off the effects of something

stamina—the ability to continue an activity for a long time

venomous—able to produce venom; venom is a kind of poison made by some snakes.

TO LEARN MORE

AT THE LIBRARY

Adamson, Thomas K. *Anaconda vs. Jaguar*. Minneapolis, Minn.: Bellwether Media, 2020.

Boutland, Craig. *King Cobra*. Minneapolis, Minn.: Bearport Publishing Company, 2021.

Downs, Kieran. *Wolverine vs. Honey Badger*. Minneapolis, Minn.: Bellwether Media.: 2021.

ON THE WEB

FACTSURFER

Factsurfer.com gives you a safe, fun way to find more information.

1. Go to www.factsurfer.com

2. Enter "king cobra vs. mongoose" into the search box and click Q.

3. Select your book cover to see a list of related content.

INDEX

Africa, 8

antivenom, 13

Asia, 4, 7, 8

attacks, 15, 16, 18, 19

bites, 4, 11, 12, 18, 19, 20

bodies, 7, 8, 13, 16

color, 7, 8

enemies, 16, 17, 19

Europe, 8

fangs, 10, 12

fight, 5, 17

fur, 8

glands, 12

habitat, 4, 6, 7, 9

hiss, 16

hood, 14, 16, 20

inject, 12

invasive species, 8

jaws, 11

mammals, 5

mouths, 10, 11

prey, 10, 11, 12, 15, 18

range, 4, 6, 7, 8, 9

reptiles, 4

size, 6, 7, 9, 10, 14, 16

snakes, 7, 13, 14, 20

speed, 15, 18

stamina, 17

strike, 15, 18, 19

teeth, 11, 20

tools, 8

venom, 7, 12, 13

weapons, 13, 14